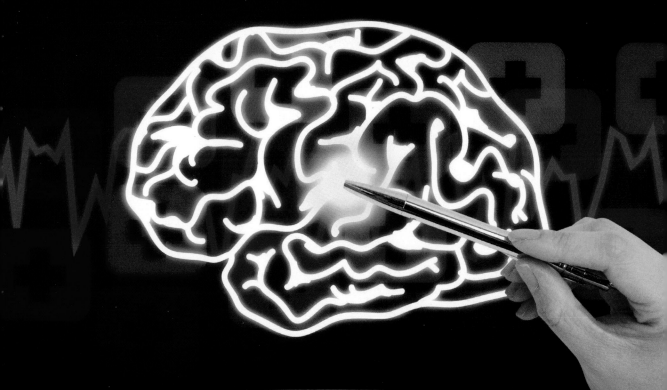

All About Your
BRAIN

Jane P. Gardner and Maria Koran

www.av2books.com

MEDIA ENHANCED BOOKS
AV²
BY WEIGL™
ADDED VALUE • AUDIO VISUAL

AV² provides enriched content that supplements and complements this book. Weigl's AV² books strive to create inspired learning and engage young minds in a total learning experience.

Your AV² Media Enhanced books come alive with...

Audio
Listen to sections of the book read aloud.

Key Words
Study vocabulary, and complete a matching word activity.

Video
Watch informative video clips.

Quizzes
Test your knowledge.

Embedded Weblinks
Gain additional information for research.

Slide Show
View images and captions, and prepare a presentation.

Go to www.av2books.com, and enter this book's unique code.

BOOK CODE

G 3 7 7 8 2 8

Try This!
Complete activities and hands-on experiments.

... and much, much more!

AV² by Weigl brings you media enhanced books that support active learning.

Published by AV² by Weigl
350 5th Avenue, 59th Floor
New York, NY 10118
Website: www.av2books.com

Library of Congress Cataloging-in-Publication Data

Names: Gardner, Jane P., author.
Title: Brain / Jane P. Gardner and Maria Koran.
Description: New York, NY : AV2 by Weigl, [2017] | Series: All about your...
  | Includes bibliographical references and index.
Identifiers: LCCN 2016034627 (print) | LCCN 2016035180 (ebook) | ISBN
  9781489651310 (hard cover : alk. paper) | ISBN 9781489651327 (soft cover :
  alk. paper) | ISBN 9781489651334 (Multi-user ebk.)
Subjects: LCSH: Brain--Juvenile literature. | Brain--Physiology--Juvenile
  literature.
Classification: LCC QP376 .G37 2017 (print) | LCC QP376 (ebook) | DDC
  612.8/2--dc23
LC record available at https://lccn.loc.gov/2016034627

Printed in the United States of America in Brainerd, Minnesota
1 2 3 4 5 6 7 8 9 0   20 19 18 17 16

082016
210716

Project Coordinator: Piper Whelan   Art Director: Terry Paulhus

Contents

Chapter 1
Use Your Brain

Thinking, breathing, dreaming, talking, eating, running, writing. You might do all these things today. Each action is controlled by one organ in your body, the brain. The brain is the third largest organ in the body. It uses more energy than any of the other organs.

Some people think the brain looks like a bunch of cauliflower. It is soft, wrinkly, and gray. It sits in liquid inside your skull. An adult human brain weighs about 3 pounds (1.4 kilograms).

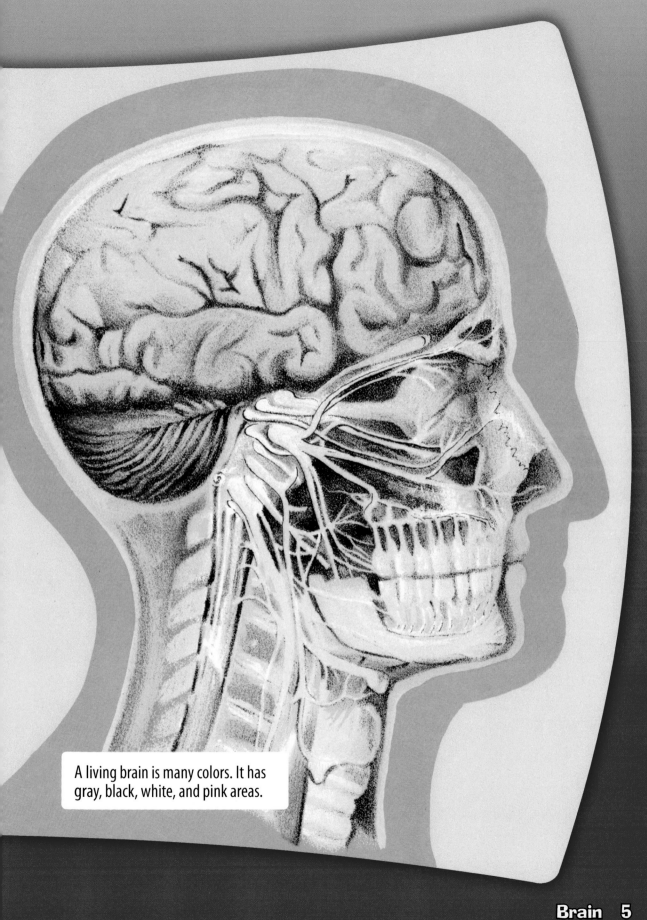

A living brain is many colors. It has gray, black, white, and pink areas.

The brain has three different parts. Each part controls different areas of your life. Some parts make you creative. Other parts help you walk and talk. Some parts of your brain keep your body at 98.6 degrees Fahrenheit (37 degrees Celsius).

The **forebrain** is the largest part of the brain. It is in the front part of your skull. This is where the **cerebrum** is located. The cerebrum controls your thoughts. It also helps you memorize spelling words and solve math problems. A lot of thinking goes on in the forebrain.

The brain is not just for thinking. It also controls how your body moves.

Are you artsy and creative, or are you more of a numbers person who likes things to be in order? Left-brain thinkers tend to be more orderly. Right-brain thinkers tend to be more artsy.

The smallest part of the brain is called the **midbrain**. The **brain stem** is part of the midbrain. The brain stem controls your breathing. It also makes sure your **involuntary** muscles do their job. These are the muscles that work all on their own. Your heart is an involuntary muscle. You do not have to think about your heart beating because it beats by itself.

Can you dribble a basketball or play the piano? You can do these things because of your **hindbrain**. The hindbrain is at the back of your skull. This part of the brain includes the **cerebellum**. The cerebellum controls the way your body moves. It helps you balance on a beam or sit up straight in your chair.

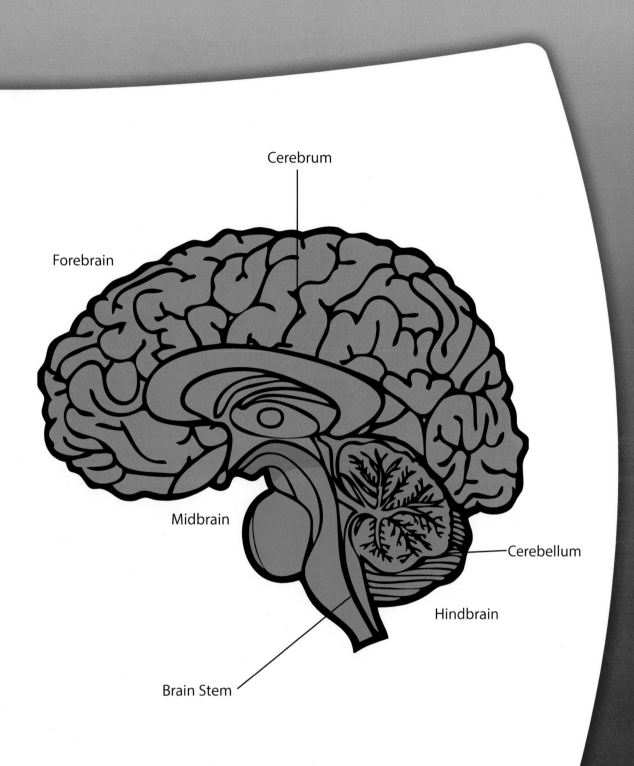

Cerebrum

Forebrain

Midbrain

Cerebellum

Hindbrain

Brain Stem

Chapter 2
What Does the Brain Do?

The brain and the spinal cord make up the **central nervous system**. Without them, you would not be able to act or think. **Neurons** are like messengers to the central nervous system. The neurons collect information from different parts of the body. Then, they bring these messages to your brain.

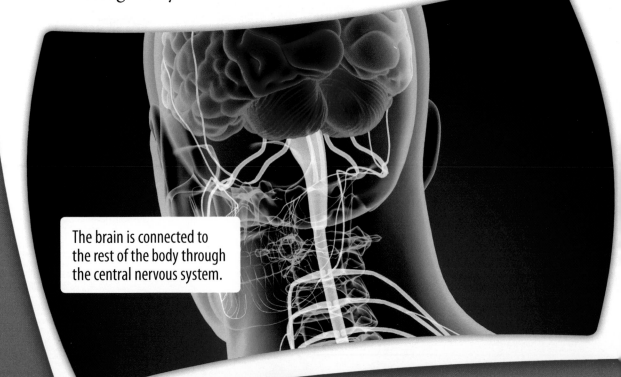

The brain is connected to the rest of the body through the central nervous system.

The brain can remember things you were just told, as well as things from a long time ago. Even a song heard once can be remembered by the brain.

If you put your hand on something hot, the neurons in your hand send messages to your brain. The brain thinks about those messages and sends a message back to your hand. The message tells your hand to move off the hot object. All of this happens in less than one second.

Your brain has more than 86 billion neurons. Neurons help you balance on your bike and remember the words to your favorite song.

Your brain helps you learn new things. Every time you learn something new, your brain changes a little bit. Maybe you wonder why your teacher always tells you to study, or why your coach always tells you to practice. This is because practice teaches our brains how to do something new.

Think of tying your shoes. You did not know how to tie them when you were younger. After practicing, you now can tie your shoes almost without looking. Every time you practiced, your brain sent messages to your hands about tying your shoes. These messages traveled the same path over and over until you learned how to tie your shoes. Now your brain does not really have to think about it. Your brain already knows the "shoe-tying" path to follow.

About 70,000 thoughts pass through your brain every day. Your brain keeps working even when you sleep.

Learning new things is fun and also keeps your brain active and healthy.

Chapter 3

Problems with the Brain

The brain is inside your skull. An adult human skull is about 1/4 inch (7 millimeters) thick. A few layers of soft tissue and fluid are around the brain. The skull, layers of tissue, and fluid all help protect the brain from injuries.

You cannot break your brain like you can break your arm or your finger, but your brain can still get injured. A common brain injury is a **concussion**. This is when the brain moves inside the skull after a hit or a fall. Concussions can happen if you get hit too hard while playing football or if you take a bad fall off your bike. Someone with a concussion might feel confused, sleepy, or sick. Someone who might have a concussion should see a doctor right away.

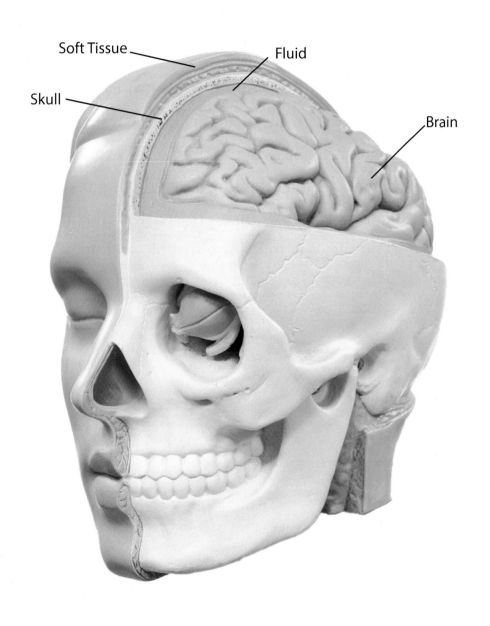

Soft Tissue

Fluid

Skull

Brain

Sometimes cells in the brain grow in weird ways. This can form a brain tumor. Most tumors cause problems. A tumor grows on a part of the brain. As it grows bigger, it pushes on the brain to try to make room for itself. The part the tumor is growing on can change. If a tumor is pushing on the part of the brain that helps you see, you may have trouble seeing.

When you have a headache, it is your head that hurts, not your brain. The brain cannot sense or feel any pain.

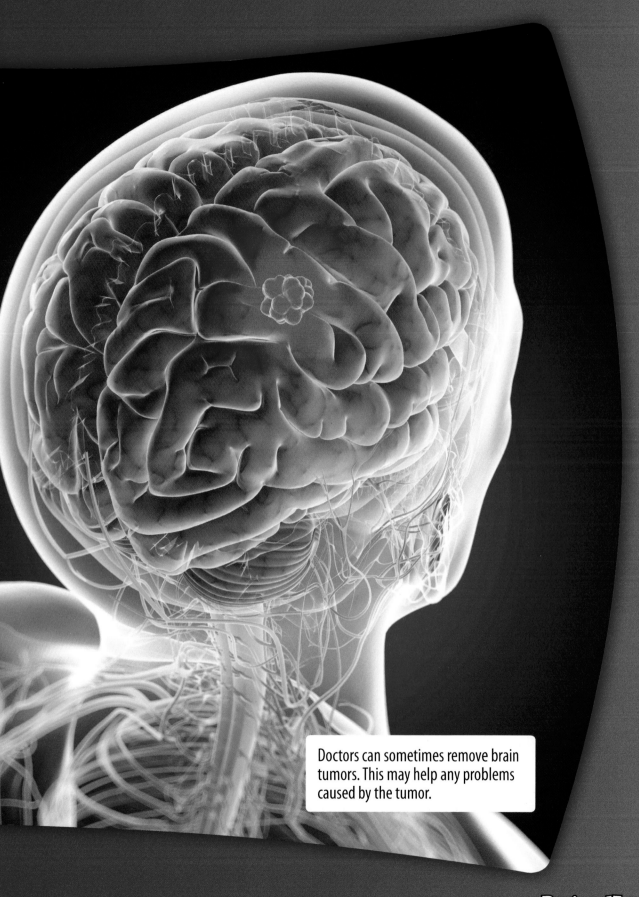

Doctors can sometimes remove brain tumors. This may help any problems caused by the tumor.

Chapter 4

Keep Your Brain Healthy

Everyone needs to keep his or her brain healthy and safe. There are many ways to keep your brain in tip-top shape.

Eat healthy foods. Fish is sometimes called "brain food." Fish, such as tuna and salmon, have chemicals that keep the brain healthy. Other foods that are good for the brain include dark fruits and vegetables, such as raisins and spinach. Nuts, such as walnuts, pecans, and almonds, are also part of a good diet for the brain.

Get plenty of exercise. Being active can help keep your brain in good shape. It is important to be safe when you exercise or play a sport. Always wear a helmet when riding a bike or a scooter. Make sure the helmet is the right size for your head. The straps should fit tight and snug under your chin.

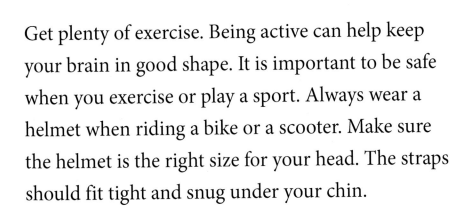

Wearing protective head gear can help to prevent an injury.

Some poisons can damage the brain. **Carbon monoxide** is a gas you cannot see or smell. It can come from the gas we use for heaters or cars. It mixes in with the air we breathe. We are around small amounts of carbon monoxide all the time. Too much can damage the brain. Help keep the brains in your home healthy. Ask your parents to make sure gas heaters in your home are working as they should.

Be curious about the world around you. Reading, writing, and playing games are all good things to do every day. Ask more questions. Learning new things and solving problems can help keep your brain healthy.

Reading is great exercise for the brain.

Get to bed early tonight. Studies show students do better on math problems with a good night's sleep.

Quiz

1. **How much does an adult human brain weigh?**

2. **What is the largest part of the brain?**

3. **What part of the brain controls your thoughts?**

4. **Where is the cerebellum found?**

5. **What does the brain stem control?**

6. **How many thoughts pass through your brain each day?**

7. **What system do the brain and spinal cord make up?**

8. **What is a concussion?**

9. **Why is fish sometimes called "brain food"?**

10. **How are neurons like messengers to the central nervous system?**

Answers

1. About 3 pounds (1.4 kilograms)
2. The forebrain
3. The cerebrum
4. In the hindbrain
5. Breathing and the involuntary muscles
6. About 70,000
7. The central nervous system
8. A brain injury that happens when the brain moves inside the skull after a hit or a fall
9. It has chemicals that keep the brain healthy
10. They collect information from different parts of the body and bring this information to the brain

Key Words

brain stem: the connection between the brain and the spinal cord

carbon monoxide: a poisonous gas made by vehicles and other things that burn fuel

central nervous system: the part of the nervous system made up of the brain and the spinal cord

cerebellum: the part of the brain that helps with balance

cerebrum: the part of the forebrain that controls body movement and collects information from the senses

concussion: a brain injury caused by a hard hit to the head

forebrain: the largest part of the brain, located in the front part of the skull

hindbrain: the part of the brain at the back of the skull

involuntary: done automatically or without control

midbrain: the smallest part of the brain, containing the brain stem

neurons: cells that carry information between the brain and other body parts

Index

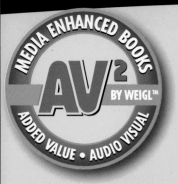

Log on to www.av2books.com

AV[2] by Weigl brings you media enhanced books that support active learning. Go to www.av2books.com, and enter the special code found on page 2 of this book. You will gain access to enriched and enhanced content that supplements and complements this book. Content includes video, audio, weblinks, quizzes, a slide show, and activities.

AV[2] Online Navigation

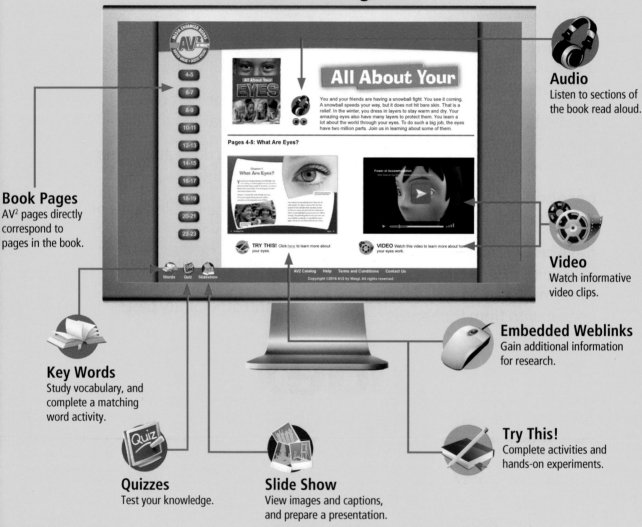

Book Pages
AV[2] pages directly correspond to pages in the book.

Audio
Listen to sections of the book read aloud.

Video
Watch informative video clips.

Embedded Weblinks
Gain additional information for research.

Key Words
Study vocabulary, and complete a matching word activity.

Try This!
Complete activities and hands-on experiments.

Quizzes
Test your knowledge.

Slide Show
View images and captions, and prepare a presentation.

AV[2] was built to bridge the gap between print and digital. We encourage you to tell us what you like and what you want to see in the future.

Sign up to be an AV[2] Ambassador at www.av2books.com/ambassador.